TONGUES TIED

Written by Lauren Ducrey
Illustrations by Erwan de Beauchaine
Creative Direction by Supereasy Studio

Made (with love) in the Spring-Summer of 2021
In NYC, Paris, and on the road

"They padded their way into adulthood;
growing up, they learned to line what they felt."

To all the kids inside grown bodies who have a lot to say,
but don't always know how.

TABLE OF CONTENTS

ITCHY HEELS

After walking out the glass doors
with a fresh breeze that makes my heels click,

I turn right
into the fast waning sun

towards which I deliberately march
beating the snare drum of its last hours

with hooved feet itching to scamper straight
down my favorite diagonal;

I dart from my big 14th street building block
and head body first downtown,

as setting rays graze the rolling pastures of my grin before
dipping into dimples of delight

that tug at the corners
of my mouth, full

with an appetite whetted by humid streets
into which these tootsies on a roll take juicy bites

or rather, nibble at with a precise, clinical hunger
to get lost

demoted from being
me, promoted to being anybody

striding for the pleasure of adventure
and anonymity,

but I don't, get lost:
I always end up finding what I was looking for

in yet another Chinatown shop
into which I wander, without fail in wonder

and cruise down shelved avenues;
my heels click their lips

smacking of dirty soles, soy sauce
and solitary strolls.

SELF-PORTRAIT AS A TALL PERSON

As a tall person

I could reach the can of olives
on the very top shelf at the grocery store.

No balancing act on an upside down shopping basket turned
stepping stool,
a miniature polymer stage, pliable and highly unreliable.

No fear of slipping off the tip of my toes and knocking down 56
glass jars of 7 dollar olives that will undoubtedly domino into
the oil section and unleash an extra virgin tsunami frothing with
shame and stuttering apologies.

Every time I stare up at the holy grail
salty, pitted and packaged

I am invested with a mission
to ask an average sized soul

if they might be so kind as to please
grab two of the store-brand cans for me

you see I am what is politely call "petite"
and surprisingly, being crowned with a French adjective

doesn't elevate me high enough to reach
what I can't.

I measure cans and cannots in inches and
feet

mine are only a size six
I used to feel sick with shyness.

Some days
the lack of highness

commands I stick out a hand
wave at a grocery shopping man

"Would you mind?"
"Sure."

As simple as syrup.
The silver lining of my shiny can
gleams on my face:

I do not smile with the satisfaction of my prize
nor bear teeth in anticipation of the perfect appetizer both juicy
and firm that makes me feel sorry for the sorry lost souls who
"hate olives, like, I can't even be around them" you must also
hate kittens and the soft caress of Sunday morning sunlight.
No, I grin

at the flavor of asking and
tasting a response

of stretching not upwards but

outwards

and receiving a hand.
Asking for one isn't as painful as it sounds.

I already have two, but three is company
especially when you feel tiny.

Some days,
I give up.

I look up longingly at the olives,
an inverted Juliet.

I realize, this is how Romeo must have felt,
hands and heart dangling.

But I do not climb the wall
of silence.

Most days,
I walk along its towering line

that I sheepishly toe.
Gagged by its thickness and height,

hidden in plain sight,
muted in both grocery store neons and daylight,

I live in the deafening pitch
of this self-made rampart and

most days,
hungry words break knuckles on its bricks.

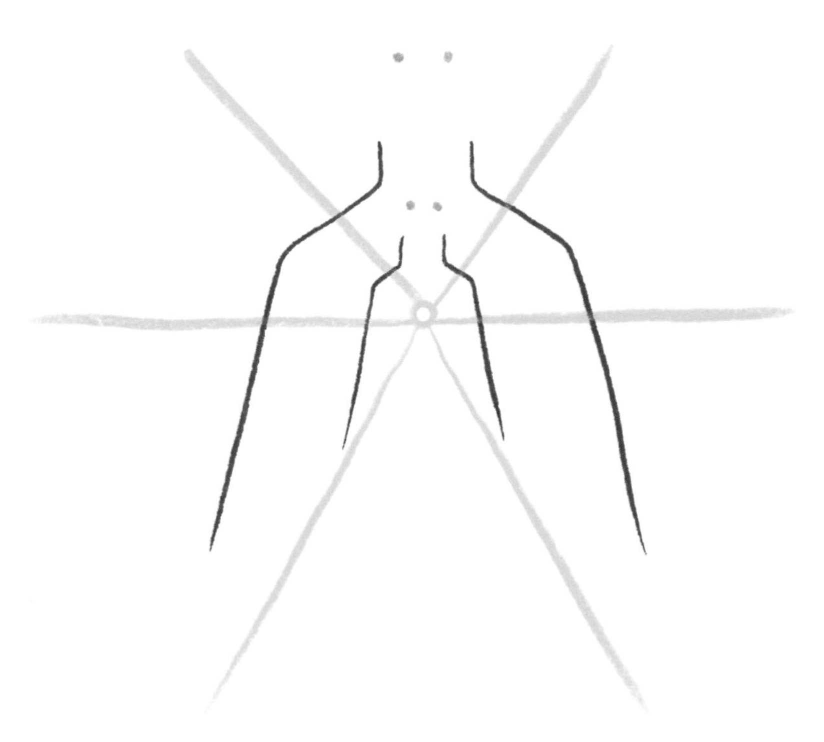

A MIND LEFT
□ UNCHECKED

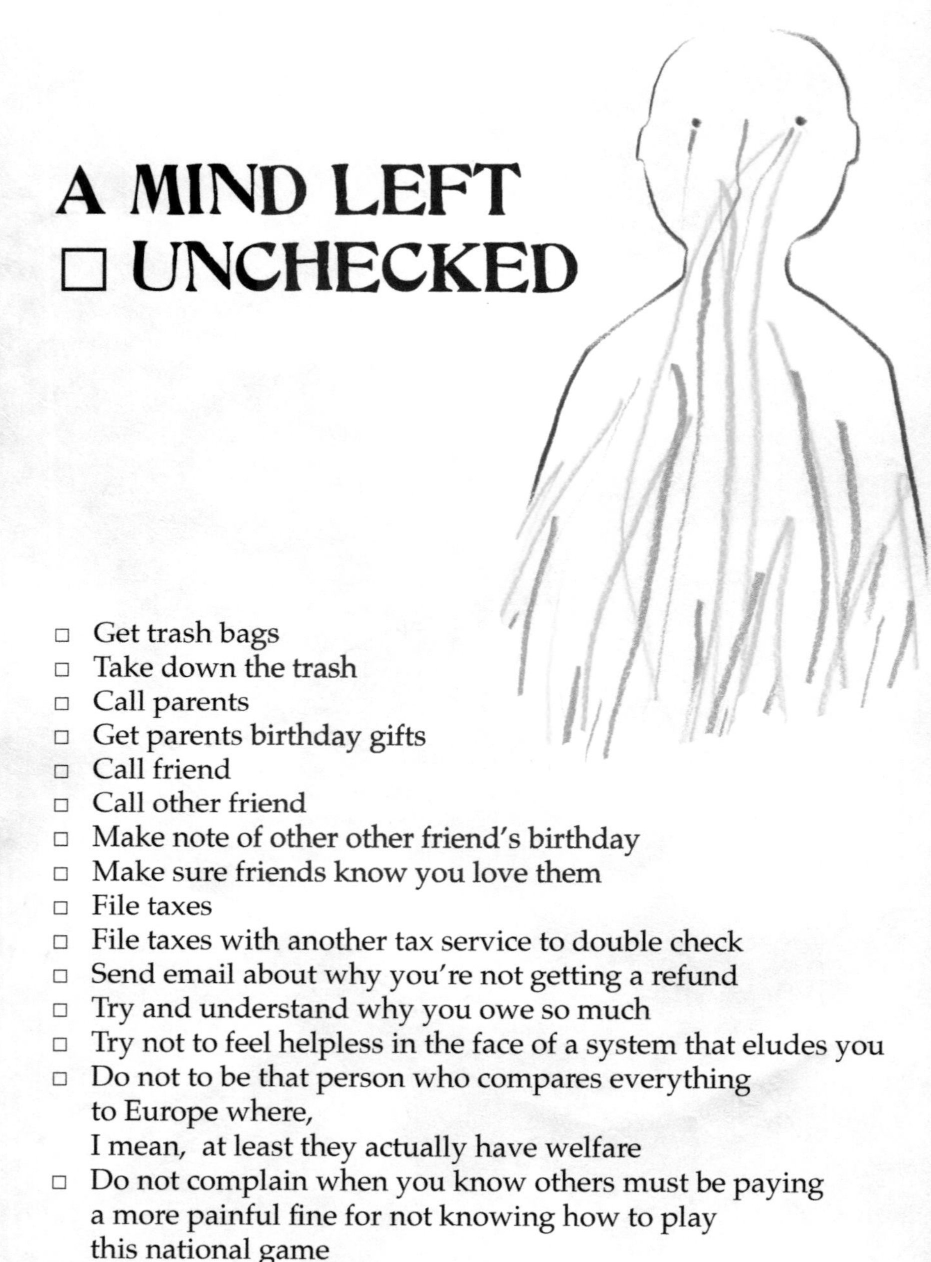

- □ Get trash bags
- □ Take down the trash
- □ Call parents
- □ Get parents birthday gifts
- □ Call friend
- □ Call other friend
- □ Make note of other other friend's birthday
- □ Make sure friends know you love them
- □ File taxes
- □ File taxes with another tax service to double check
- □ Send email about why you're not getting a refund
- □ Try and understand why you owe so much
- □ Try not to feel helpless in the face of a system that eludes you
- □ Do not to be that person who compares everything
  to Europe where,
  I mean, at least they actually have welfare
- □ Do not complain when you know others must be paying
  a more painful fine for not knowing how to play
  this national game
- □ Renew driver's license at the DMV
- □ Note that you lost your social security card
- □ Don't forget to take your American passport to the airport
  this week

- □ Remind yourself where both your French
  and American passports are
- □ Remember they're the most valuable property you own,
- □ even more so now you're down
  two other printed pieces of evidence of your existence
- □ Go and check they're actually where you thought
- □ They are
- □ You knew this
- □ Yet the paranoid sense of administrative precarity
  summoned the voice of doubt
  that only a sleek tick on a to do list
  could gag
- □ Learn to quiet the deafening emptiness
- □ of an unchecked box
- □ Fragile, handle carefully but
- □ try and wrestle with the belief
  that leaving even but one box untouched
  exposes a gaping hole through which time
  leaks

unproductive

□ opportunities

slip

squandered

□ happiness

remains just beyond

reach,

□ wasted

and the fear of future seeps corrosive

□ Just write poetry
with line
breaks
and give yourself
one

□ Remember to embrace empty spaces

DEMOTED FROM

BEING

ME, PROMOTED TO

BEING ANYBODY

A WINTER STRAIGHTJACKET

I can't sleep
less isn't more
in this case
wine won't help
I'm already drowning
in a beating chest   it dawns
on both the snow and   me
that warm feelings have frozen over
into a petrified
                              panic

I wear a winter straightjacket
woven from
                    unravelling
                         strings
I am told should be

unattached

"Sorry, I can't"
And yet we did
ride through the night
once frivolous with insomnia
spinning our bike wheels
until an alkaline sun gushed
over the desert's bleached rim
bare unpretentious dreamscape

A big dog breathes deeply

Stolen glances crowd thoughts again
embraces suffocate when held too long
like this night
sleep
lest
the
confusion of
dreams
seep
into a feverish morning

PETRIFIED* PAST

Weak nights are the stuff of strong liquor.

Fragile dances around doorsteps
Soft conversations side stepped
Harsh thoughts hushed
Dry leaves crushed, parched
discussions ambushed
by a gust of wandering wind.

Last call, phones ring unanswered.
Glassy-eyed, I leave a ring
stain behind and a glass half full.

A net of neurons pearls
into beads that thread thoughts.

It captures enrapturing constructs
of men that cannot matter:
they are made
only of grey matter.

* **Pet•ri•fy** ('petrə,fī) *v.* **To change organic matter into a stony concretion by encrusting or replacing its original substance with a calcareous, siliceous, or other mineral deposit.**

Forged memories
brand my brain,
a relentless blacksmith
strikes copper past

into iron present.

YELLOW CONFETTI

The branches erupt with yellow confetti,
celebratory shreds of summer
tossed up in a whirlwind
of festive
        falling:
one last hurrah before
branches lay bare
as we do, under layers of knitted armour.

I toot a broken party horn
to distract the thought of cleaning up
all these tiny
little
pieces
that have fallen through the cracks ,
but the wind covers the sound in a flare
and leaves me naked, bearing unfitted *amour*.

DAYLIGHT SHAVINGS

The leaves on my houseplant turn yellow in a day
a desperate dash to follow suit
with all the unhoused plants
outside.

My lips chap, skin cracks.

The clock strikes back
an hour,
somehow running circles around the sun,
a significantly more senior time-keeper.

I stare helpless as the leaves shed
my skin, feet planted
roots tingle with time:
Am I an air plant
or the white floating skeleton of a dandelion ?

THE FIRST LETTER OF THE ALPHABET IS I

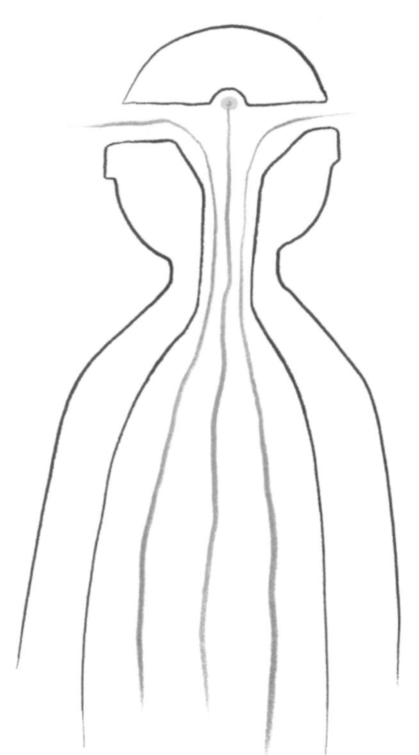

i.
They weren't dyslexic.

They had simply grown up learning
the wrong alphabet;
were taught that "you"
is spelled e-g-o

that the first letter of the alphabet is
I.

I am am am

ii.
As soon as eyes blink
the world open,
the mind's I stirs
and stares.

Squadrons of thoughts march
down the backside
of fatigued eye sockets.

I want to decapitalize
the monolith.

iii.
Strangler figs are vines that grow upon host trees they eventually smother. Thirsty for sunshine the strangler seeks only to climb - it does not feed off its prop. However, it may outcompete it, replacing the old trunk with a new lattice of blind, braided hunger.
Natural mummification.

iiii.
Is I, the ego, a cursive strangler tree
so bent on survival it
petrifies life itself?

iiiii.
One trunk replaces another. I is another.
What is, is not what ought to be, what ought to be, is not what is.
A weed is
an undesired plant.
Its definition hinges on the decision
to cultivate it
or not.

iiiii.
Fatigued eye sockets flutter,
focus on the tired metaphor of man as gardener.
I shall learn to tend to the i,
let in light to feed it what it needs.
The mirage lies in its singularity,
it hides a forest -
hear the fanning of loud leaves.

i are are are

AN INSTRUMENT OF BREATH AND BONES

1.

At the age of 29,
she learned that

breathing is hard.

Remembered that as a child she had known.
She hadn't known,
she simply had,
breathed.

Unapologetically ravenous for air,
her belly used to defy gravity;
a drum, thirsty for resonance,
ribs expanding, uncaged,
rippling beneath skin
teeth sucking in breath
in the expectant swirl of a shout, an excited scream
or
to usher in the loud silence
that punctuates a gasp of awe.

She had forgotten the depth of her body,
shortened her range,
lived off of small sips
taken with shy lips.

At the age of 29
she learned that
she should breathe like she drinks water:
gallons at a time.

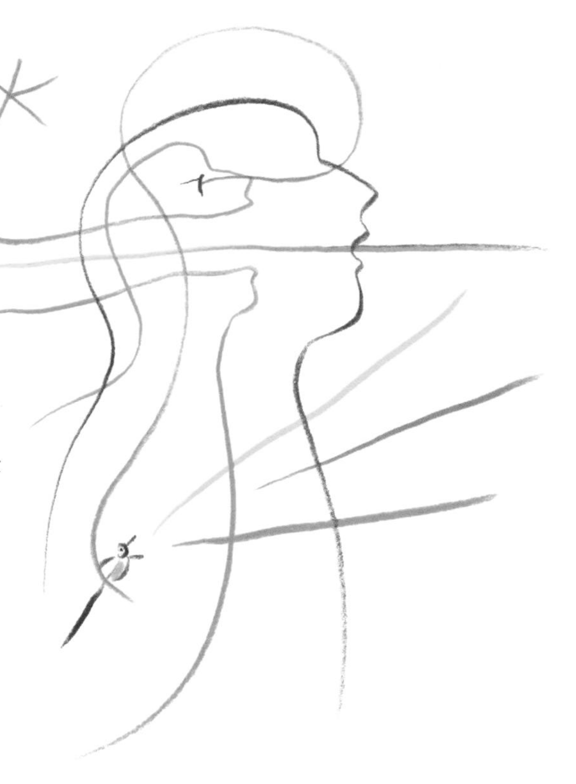

2.

She sang
A tune floated up
from stomach lungs throat

She'd sang it before
It had sung her before

Lifted up through the air
a thread, strung

Her mouth
a needle threaded

Notes sewed
skirts out of thin air,
unhemmed her insides
that fluttered with the tickle of vocal chords

There was something eternal about the air —
she recognized the unnamable quality of folk song
a melody that comes from nowhere
and speaks to everything
She mused with the idea
of this being the voice of the Earth
or whatever capitalized word
people use to speak of That which we all know is
out there

Is In Here

☞

That which all writing just fails to outline with letters
and punctuation
That to which all music tries dances to
which all art brushes upon, sculpts into, builds for, composes
with, pencils through, hums for, blueprints and choreographs
around

A ribbon lifted
unravelled her spine

Creased
Soft
Untethered

This sound that had made her before
rose again,
she struggled gently
against the tensing
against the calcified fear whose layers
seemed to peel endlessly

Befriend it,
they say

She said ok,
remembering what they say

They
all of those who touched her where the mineral deposits ossify
that got their fingers ashen with her internal debris
that fumbled kind hands on petrified insides
and helped her feel that what feels like rock
is sometimes only chalk

She said ok
Turned her attention from where it
tightened

to everywhere around
to nowhere really
and opened her mouth

let sound dissolve a scab
of skin that once needed healing
that once needed less feeling

The small tremors make
crusts crumble for a moment

For a moment she bathes it in an emanation
of acoustics and air

The memory of a tune has its own agency

She was afraid she wouldn't remember
Her mind twitched realizing she didn't know how to write
music
but the memory of a tune has its own agency
in that moment it returned
had never left
was always there to be strung

Where do notes come from
Where do they live when they're not sung

She realized the air around her was always pregnant with her
voice

and all the music

There for the plucking

The body
an instrument of breath and bones

A GIVEN MOMENT

My fingers trace the outlines of you
neat picket fences of atoms ground your outer rim.

Unsure, I gravitate around the event horizon
of the mess of flesh that pulls in light and
myself with delight.

Space opened
up a vacuum
into which
we both softly slipped
and sat
chatting for hours.

Time stood still
on the sill
of unsealed lips.

Wending words
have a way
of winding linear time
into a bow of now,
into a given moment.

THE CASE FOR GETTING DISTRACTED

The city buzzes with the onset of summer.
Warm air extends an invitation to exist in larger spaces;
the scent of hot cement
infuses a smile on my wintered face and
the urban multiverse with endless possibilities.

Perhaps I get distracted by an oncoming body
that shifts anticipated
trajectories,
defies gravity with the lightness of a word;
an address, a comet enters my personal ozone —
3, 2, 1
impact

"Excuse me, do you..."

This new orbit pulls me to another cross street
bends the continuum of an evening commute
space-time
shifts
at the speed of a lighter lent to spark cigarettes that warp into
conversations expanding faster than expected.

Or perhaps someone asks for directions -
only a brief   blip   in the course I carry on
Yet a momentary   pause
suspending the
                    unraveling
                              line of
                                   time.

Or perhaps a man hole suddenly yawns, steaming
I circle it, bump into someone new
tumble into another
                        wormhole

                                     "Excuse me, I..."

Relative coordinates try and always fail
to triangulate uncoordinated dates with strangers
that begin halfway to the subway
and end at a crosswalk.

These white stripes paint milky
ways on the city's surface
for ships to pass in the night,
for multiple verses to collide.

Or perhaps as the train pulls out of the station
my attention stumbles on
someone's dimples;
a person I've already seen
and never noticed comes
into   focus.

☞

The moon is a bright white rock
until my mind draws a face on it,
bearing a smile I cannot unsee:
when my attention lands
on you
I know this small wink is a great stamp
on the course of my memories.

I wonder how many times we glided
over the same noisy tracks
traveled at the same time from home
to wherever we go and back.

If two asteroids are unknowingly on the same path
is it synchronicity
or mere chance
in a world where time is only ever really manifest
through entropy?

The growing chaos I know to be a rule of our universe
is perhaps the ultimate revolt against determinacy,
against the idea there is anything less than miraculous
for me to see you
and you, to notice me.

As this train of thought
blazes ahead at warp speed,
I trip
and wonder how many other people here
harbor the potentiality
of connecting to a whole new reality?
The fractured tree of present possibilities
makes me dizzy,
time
collapses
vertically
and from its vertiginous heights I feel dazed
unsteady

"Excuse me, but what if..."

Or
perhaps I fumble
for a few words, an address, a comet
that collides with your smile,
which flashes with the flicker of stars so far
they've already died.

"Excuse me: hi."

I still myself
to distill coincidence into a moment
indivisible and highly visible.

Because perhaps when I step into syzygy
with your celestial body,
it dawns on me that there is nowhere to fall
but head over heels
in the light tug of your gravity.

THE SYNTAX OF YOUR GAZE

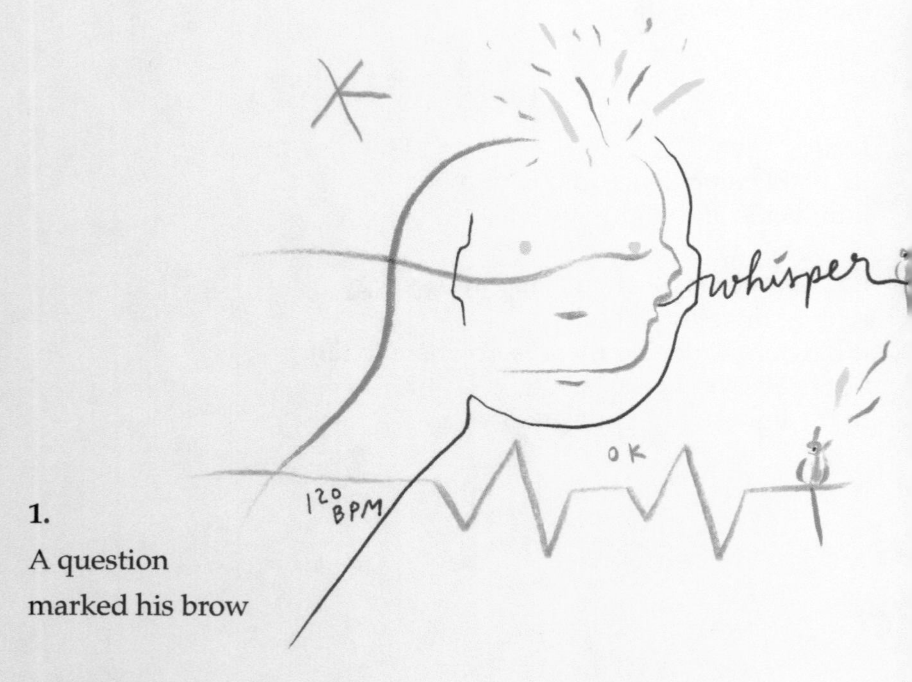

1.

A question
marked his brow

lifted,
a bow ready to shoot.

I layed down my arms
around his neck

and realized

his attention
was directed towards me, not
an arrow.

2.

Your truth lies
like the silent
t
of listen:

quiet, central, implicit.

An anchoring of words
often mispronounced by those
alien to your ways.
It lies
present between the lines
that harden on your face
when threatened
by the barbarity of
communication.

Your glare
two pinholes
from which no light escapes,
holds it captive.

☞

Yet a soft throb,
its delicate pulse,
ripples over tears
rarely shed.

I learn to interpret the punctuation
of your body.

The furrow in your brow
a hyphen - a stitch
an olive branch
rather than a barrier
spells out concern
to better understand.

I learn to read the grammar
of your demeanor.

The purse of your lips
conjugates the present, tense
into a future more perfect.
It speaks words of silence
signifying not judgment
but respect.

I learn to translate the syntax
of your face.

The blank stare not a stone wall
but a protective canvas masking
confused feelings.
It writes an open clause,
careful to not jump
to a close.

I learn to tune into
the phonetics
of your thoughts.

The assertive tone
an invitation to harmonize
into conversation;
it sings not counter arguments
but rather a *contre-point*.

Your truth lies
like the silent
t
of soften:

necessary, tall, deafeningly still
in the middle of it all.

Your truth relies
on me
to learn
and read.

YOUR
TRUTH
LIES
LIKE
THE
SILENT

T
OF
LISTEN

CROSS SWELL

Two weather systems that are far from each other may create a cross sea when the waves from the systems meet at a place far from either weather system. Although they create a perilous sea hazard for seafarers, the aesthetics of the phenomenon are remarkable.

Why?

A double edged word.

Why.

A mind can both wield
curious enquiry
and
inquisitive demand.

The sound of sincerity sometimes
rings off key -
a voice slips
Freudian
crystal breaks, out of tune.

My mind is a coin
I no longer want to flip

eyes closed, fingers crossed,
hoping it lands on tails
rather than on the head of an argument.

Why.

Control cloaked in a question

misses the mark, hits soft flesh,
pangs with pain inflamed
by duplicitous words
well intentioned
heavy with tension.

When you argue the orange is
green
let me ask

why?

Let me candidly inspect
the unfolding of perception,
how you peel back thick skin;

listen

to the crinkle
of things unwrapped:

an angry ball of paper?
or an origami of thought.

Layers of intricately pleated paper
reveal a map of the world I know not
how to read:
it must be felt.
A soft fumble finds meridians
drawn from scars,
hugged by an equator of fear.
Twenty thousand leagues under
I see the crust of your core crest
with the beat of affection.

Anchors with teeth dug deep
rust, solitary in endless tides.
Instead of trying
to make the compass point
in my direction
let me let it spin for both of us
to meet in the middle of
where we've never been.
When two waves converge their ripples braid the sea.

TONGUES

Her mouth was pregnant.
with i love yous

stillborn on the sill
of sealed lips.

Swallowing her words
always left her hungry.

I listened to words.
rewrite his face into
a stranger.

Their stain lasted long
after the argument ended.

TIED

Elle avait la bouche pleine
d'une compote de « je t'aime »
dont la saveur s'etait estompée
à force de trop mâcher ses mots.

Les couleuvres
sont moins dures à avaler.

Je le regardais
devenir inconnu,

ses traits tordus
par les volutes de notre dispute.

Les mots ne decrivent pas les autres,
ils les recrivent.

PADDING

1.
They padded their way into adulthood;
growing up, they learned to line what they felt.

They wore skins hemmed with velvet,
cotton and indifference
to soften the blows
of winds that bite from the inside,
to dull the needles of feelings.

2.
She had 20/20 vision
but like many, she suffered from myopic insight.

Her eyelids drew up barriers
past which the strange patterns of her mind
failed to map to a world
others could read.

She learned that her uniqueness
was illusion cloaked in shame.

"I thought I was the only weird one to think that."

She gladfully shook it off
and took a naked stride,
showing the same skin
everyone else was sewn from.

3.
She stripped her skin
peeled its sleeves and pants
bloody flesh laid bare.

She felt the freshness and bite
of a nakedness she'd never experienced.

Organs skull eyeballs
ligaments veins muscles pulsing
a knotted mess of flesh and bone
instinctively disgusting
absurd to behold.

Exposed,
she faced him,
hands reached out
wet with her blood
tender yet trusting
of his touch.

"May you find wholeness
May you find peace
May you find purpose,
Just as I wish to"
She spoke borrowed words that communed
without sound.

Her hands rested on his palms
smudged with her insides
their foreheads in an embrace
eyes closed to eye socket bared
skull to skin
her content touching his lining -

They turned and began walking.

With each step
a soft membrane began
blurring the outlines
of her rawness
began holding her microcosm
with a new unfinished embrace -

FORFEITING LIFE AT A FUNERAL

Forget to get toilet paper, use tissues instead.
Forget to buy milk, black coffee spanks you out of bed.
Forget to do the laundry, holey socks hide skillfully in sneakers.
Forget to do the laundry again: you're a natural born streaker.

Forget to fetch the mail, childhood's holy grail.
Forget your umbrella; it's eloped with all the single socks, cheeky fella.
Forget to lock the door, hackers only pick at firewalls anymore.
Forget your phone at home and sever limb and bone
- or maybe a leash?

Forget the text you wish you hadn't sent.
Forget it like the texts you once sent and can't remember.
Forget the text your never sent.
Three dots rolling in a loop
...
Drops of digital water torture.
Forget you're a persecutor by proxy server.
Forget about him.
Actually, forget that and focus on
forgetting the story you spun and tangled in
when you tied up memories into a clean bow
and laced a noose instead.
Forging the past is an unpleasant present.

Forget the argument you didn't win.
Forget doubts downed with each drink.
"Forget it," you said and walked away.
With each sip you replay the scene
until it's bloated and obscene.

The kiss, the grin, the glance,
the touch, the jesting, the suggestion,
the compliment, the contemplation, the physical temptation,
taser memory with masochistic melancholy.
Forgetfulness is ignorance reclaimed is bliss.
Forgetfulness deflates regret with a hiss.
Or
forgetfulness is letting go of something you won't miss.

So forget about trying to remember your whole shopping list
like trying to stuff a sleeping bag into a sack that never fits.
Forget freely and trust a tug on a thought will string the rest
along.
Forget just enough, to remember vividly what's left.

Forget meaning, remember foraged skin.
Forgive moments for being fleeting.
Forgetting is forfeiting life at a funeral:
Formal surrender to the limits of being.

SHE
REALIZED
THE
AIR
AROUND
HER

WAS
ALWAYS
PREGNANT
WITH
HER
VOICE

I NEVER QUITE
GET USED
TO THE SUDDEN
NOTHINGNESS
OF ENDINGS

Thank you

She breathes through solar plexus heart throat mind

They sit on a stoop
with the heavy lightness of an ending
with simple words
empty hangers balancing on the edge of lips
a closet laid bare
a wind of all the clothes and masks they had once torn off
tugs at the heart and the corners of her mouth
that turn down in a shiver of sadness

Thank you

A column of clouds grounds her
with warm air
a balloon in her breast

How easily the sand bags of resentment
try and climb their way in
one last punch
one last shot at the corn hole —

but Thank you

gently sifts debris into the breeze
through open fingers
a fist unclenched
hands that would no longer hold, fingers unbraided

It's a beautiful day
They've emptied it
to the last sip

They sit and say they have a new thirst to quench
She has a sink inside
He has a bottle in his bag
They won't clink cups
they will each soothe a parched throat

☞

Thank you

their silent separate cheer

Thank you

she feels the words deeply for
The trust
The patience
The sharing
The unbearing
The touch
The opening of her origami body
The unravelling of her mind
It had hurt to pull on knotted threads but it had unkinked
some of her colors that no longer bleed
so dark, coagulated
no longer tie such a tight noose around her neck

Thank you for the unwavering truth spoken in such loud words

Thank you

for letting us let go
for letting me let you go
I was hurting you and you deserve never to be

Thank you for existing

Over a decade ago you told me you almost stopped
existing
and I cannot speak thicker words of thanks
for having gotten the opportunity honor joy intimacy of sharing
an orbit
for a moment

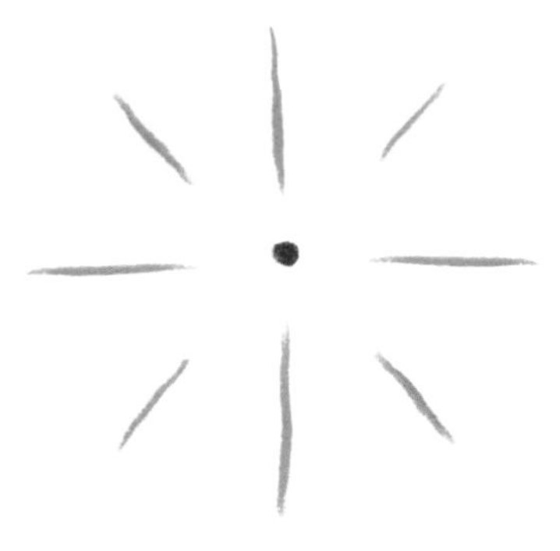

Thank you

Thank you

Thank you

MORNING YAWN

Diligent photons
carve a window on the wall across my bed.

Its brightness shakes flakes of sleep
from the curtains of my eyes;
drawn, lids let in light.

Shadows outline the first frame of the morning,
play with angles that redesign the architecture of my room:
sun rays widen 90 degree angles,
bend a rectangle into a slanted polygon -
it hovers, as if ajar onto the day which it opens.

I picture these tiny particles
building space out of invisible dimensions
my human eye can only glimpse
as a collapse of light onto the canvas that is my wall,
white, the color a net for their waves
that crash so much faster than sound.

This luminous sill shifts,
eventually sets behind my chaise.

The street's acoustics rise,
the chirping of conversations, car doors closing,
an airplane hums a familiar doppler tune.

I look up,
stunned:
on the ceiling a branch sways softly
in a breeze I cannot feel
or under the weight of a bird
I don't see.
I stare at the reflection,
of the second window that turns my perception inside out,
the world outside in,
projecting glass panes, grills, trees, leaves and all.

How does that even work?
Where does the light refract vertically?
Where does its elbow reach upwards
for it to place a palm on the roof of my room,
today's digital imprint?

The physics of it tie the ribbons of my mind
into a bow,
a package of incredible present.

I wake surrounded by windows
that yawn before they move on
to the main course of the day,
reminders that openings abund
weightlessly robust,
heedless of gravity.

A SCENT

OF

NEAR

REMINISCENT

A

FUTURE

THE PROMISE OF KNOWLEDGE

A taunting tickle.

A scent,
reminiscent of a
near future.

A fleeting déjà-not-yet-vu
on the tip
of the brain's tongue —

my mind's epidermis is ablaze
with the deep pleasure
of not yet understanding
Something I know
I can.

The moment of knowledge will be
Im-mediate

A quantum leap
with no trajectory
no movement;
pure emergence

impressed simultaneously by everyfiberofmybody,
all at once parchment and clerk and author of
everything I cognize
and
re-cognize.

Sense-making is
senses making sense
is sensual
is sensational.

Illustrations by Erwan de Beauchaine
Creative Direction by Supereasy Studio
Made in the Spring-Summer of 2021

Printed in the USA
CPSIA information can be obtained
at www.ICGtesting.com
LVHW062021211223
767165LV00003B/10

* 9 7 8 1 0 8 7 9 9 4 2 9 1 *